Simpatico Patio!

BY

RANDY STARK

Simpatico Patio!

First Edition September, 2005

For more information contact:
Write Up The Road Publishing
P.O. Box 69
Kenton, TN 38233
(800) 292-8072
www.writeuptheroad.com

Stark, Randy G.
Simpatico Patio!

ISBN: 0-9724026-5-9
Library of Congress Control Number: 2005923825

A Write Up The Road Book
Printed in the United States of America

Dedication

To my parents, in the arms of angels.

Simpatico Patio!

Bicycles, Bakers, and Cakes

Bicycles, Bakers, and Cakes

The bicycle went his wheel very fast trying to get that cake.
And the bicycle got that cake.
And the baker said, "Get that bicycle."
But the bicycle get to his home.
And the bicycle shut his walk.
The three bicycles---
There were *three* bicycles---eat the cake.
The baker didn't serve it either!
The bicycles serve it and eat it all up.
All the bicycles eat it all up.

A shark got near those bicycles
And bring some hair on them.
So they jumped, jumped, jumped.
All the bicycles jumped.
Then the bicycles sleeped.
Then the bicycles got some clothes on.
It was ten bicycles!
And the bicycles ride around and they saw a baker.
And they smashed a cake on their faces.
And then the bicycles swimmed in a lake.

Hurtovese

Birds and skunks in a revolving front door,
Cockroaches prefer the bathroom,
Ants have furred the kitchen and fallen into the empties.
When it gets light enough I read about
Bombs in the Bangladesh cinema,
A pyramid scheme in Egypt

Until fire from the Movement for Parti-Colored Currency
Transfers our sphincters to our socks.
I naval the c.o. at paperfort: hit and intercept niner
Four clown report to three vagisil sector vector hurtovese.
(Hurtovese is one of those words--
It means what you want it to.)

Low flying aircraft tangle in the tennis nets.
Arp arp barks the Cubist cur.
Then there's one less dog in our barrio.
Bell towers explode like paper lanterns.
You call it good sipping whiskey,
I call it hurtovese.

Es Prohibido Traer Este Poema Al Baño Durante Horas De Trabajo

Dad takes his coffee at the kitchen table
And checks in at the dream counter.
His zugunruhe is acting up.
The coffee is laced up
Like boots of finest calfskin on pretty feet and legs
Like Dad said to Mom when they first met:
"Honey, your daddy's a thief."

Mom was all
"Whatchyou mean my daddy's a thief?
My daddy ain't no thief."
Dad was all
"Honey, your daddy stole the light right out of the stars
And put it in your eyes."
(You'd be surprised what that does to a gal.)

They got married just before Dad joined the
Gravitational Force
Because it is the dominant force in our everyday life.
(Like Dad told his daughter:
"You want meat? Marry a butcher.")
And when Dad got a birthday sausage from his son-in-law
It tasted like Shamu but made him feel mighty proud,

Proud enough to start drinking at nine in the morning.
He kisses Mom and the tip of her tongue
Tickles the roof of his mouth like fine print.
He leaves for his job at the dog grooming emporium,
One eye dangling like a joke eye, the other missing,
A Glengarry of hair on his head,
For today he is expecting his favorite poodle Odette.

The Elements

"The great obstacle…was not ignorance, but the illusion of knowledge." Daniel Boorstin

Start where Harlem contests the prairie.
Uncertainty canopies a resemblance to cool being:
Like sisters spurred in baby-making rivalry.
But sometimes you need a different brand of civilization,
Or shark cartilage, or energy powder.

They arrive singly, then cluster,
Like cheese and garlic pasta pouches,
Like Black Brant geese in the eel grass,
Like that night in Tunisia when the *gusano cibernetico*
Requested a table in the smoking gun section,

Separated by the thickness of crime scene tape
From the sexiest rhizome you'll ever meet:
A flame-hipped woman with sundials for heels
Jade and obsidian dragons on her cognac suede boots glare.
She's up-to-date on her glamour shots,

Her hair is like Isaac Newton's
Only black like her heart.
She made the motorcycle-mounted assassins
Start thinking outside the dojo,
Imagining for all the world

A blind snowman smoking a crack pipe,
Cracking a knowing smile.
A blind snowman, calling for rain,
But as looters and lawyers know,
You can't prove anything without the head.

Willa Cather Slept Here

A fool's capped juggler
Unicycling the shortest distance between
Tinker toy trees,
My sleeves don't cover those tracks.
The last time I had sex was with a woman on stilts.
Silage means nothing without yield.

And for pretending to be in Paris, or
The Godfather of cyber-punk, or
The spokesperson for a generation,
I've got a tail on me like a horse in a wading pool
Even though I've been wished "good luck" by the
International boxing judge and referee

Because Willa Cather never slept here.
And for that alone I deserve to be shot
But one Pabst Blue Ribbon led to a few
And the assassin stuck his hands in the scanner
And wrote the *My Antonia*
Okra Whimsy's humping.

The Sophisticates

Damas y caballeros
Gay cafés and fucked-up friends
Tableaux many, footprints few
You can't step twice in the same milieu.

"I've been there so many times
They told me not to come back," the Queen corroborated,
Whilst pigs penned in squishy piggeries
Snorted *Symphony Number 1 in tortilla flat minor.*

By Teotihuacani tricks of physics and scale
The skies turned inconsolable.
The rain came crawling,
Crying like a baby.

The ringmaster let the big cats out of the bagpipes:
The bi-polar ice caps are melting.
That's correct. The ice caps in the bi-polar regions
Where the bi-polar bears live, they're melting.

And it didn't take eyeglasses the size of
Ceremonial ribbon cutting shears
To ascertain the eager *joi* of some incredible *vivre.*
Whilst cows played whist at the Playa Cacao.

Reservoirs filled like canteens.
Then spilled over.
"A man's hype must exceed his talent or
What's an Oscar for?"

Eggs, larvae, pupae, and adults,
Patrons of an ethnically televised neighborhood tavern,
Rising as one cocktail dress---
We laugh, we cry, we *oui oui oui* all the way home.

Great Lessons

In the Tamil section of Copenhagen
Housekeeping vomits instead of knocking,
But they clean like diamond money cleansing ethnicity
And shake out the love rugs like matadors.
The concierge conceives daily miscarriages of justice
And they say Stalin slept here. Josè Stalin.
There is sunbathing on the roof
And Spiderman climbing the fire escapes.

Right now in the lobby sipping donkey lemonade
The way it is drunk by industry types
Two helmeted youth prepping for Hajj.
The guy hasn't grown into his lips yet
She used to be his mother.
That's how they met.
They're singing canzoni like Koreans
And by dawn they're back in their room nuzzling like deer.

Housekeeping's here to prevent anybody getting off easy,
Their way of throwing a punch, like Josè "*Arcero*" Stalin.
You wonder: When is it theft? When is it innovation?
Because if you outlaw chin whiskers
Only outlaws will have chin whiskers.
Spiderman slipped and four stories later
That was the end of Spiderman
Sometimes great lessons fall right out of the blue.

Luc Truffle

You love him or you hate him.
Those with hands sit on them.
Those without applaud wildly.
Or pop Jell-O shooters.
Or play the harp.

An audible graininess pervades his early work,
An abstruse mist hissing
Like serpentine gargoyles gone out of their stone,
Like the last Maoist rebel left on Earth
Who said the heck with it and went home.

His middle period becomes a solipsism,
Shot in cartouche and subtitles
Combining the sorrow of Averroes dead in Marrakech
With the whimsy of Buñuel dining alone,
Plates piled high with nudes.

His late period is unfathomable and all that stands
Between you and the bus coming around the blind corner
Yet kept at a deceptively comfortable 298 Kelvins,
The camera's eye veined like a red-headed spider's web
Lighted by a pyre of crutches and leg braces of the healed.

He does what he does just to see the look on your face,
Like a god true to his industrial roots.
Luc calls it like he sees it.
The way Jane Goodall calls it like she sees it
And pronounces it *bubboon.*

Like A Danish Luther

Brown bag lunches with processed rainbow sandwiches,
Mamas and Papayas walking their pastiches,
Through the *jardines de la Iglesia Zapatista Bautista,*
Black bastards leashed to pink bitches,
A barrel chested cowboy in a welder's hood,
A Danish Luther playing his lute.

I took the short cut through the chopstick culture
To the *frontera* where salvage yards and residences mix
And wine is sold in milk cartons for a peso and a half.
And the pesos don't have a picture i.d.
And all sex is like sex that happens in headlights at night.
Like a Portuguese bullfight at an Odd Fellows Hall

Vagos and Hell's Angels beating each other senseless
With handlebars and tailpipes and gas tanks,
None of that art studio snobbishness like you'd find
Advancing with a four-shot non-fat latte in one hand
A Lucky 13 punched a dozen times in the other.
The next one's free!

Concerto For Pierced Piano

The fog lifts like an Alsatian chainsaw
And pimpmobiles down the draw
Scoot like ibises
All splash and lime and puffy lips
From a premium night of kissing.

Outside Innsbruck, inside Outtsbruck,
Main Street's a flight deck,
My mind astir on-a-stick.
Epsilon is my favorite Greek letter
After Señorita Caballero speaking French.

The strawberry hawks have been living a lie and
Albino canaries mistaken for home health care workers
Are killing them for their suede.
Seen from another planet through supersize telescopes
They appear to have merganser-like qualities.

At the park a man takes pictures of his pregnant wife.
Another man exposes himself to the joggers.
The species reduction act
Can't be signed into law fast enough.
Pedicabs pursuant.

Toss a buck to the wheelchaired vet
On the corner of CinemaScope and RetroSpect
She fought for your right
To choose your toilet bowl cleanser.
Hey you European primitives, I'm flying!

The Silver Dollar-Sized Pancakes
Drive-In Theater

It was the Applematics
Where Sara Lee Poundcake
Surrendered to *Ulysses* by James Joyce
After commissioners of pep fought for
The right to a gated community.
Wild asparagus couldn't stop them
Say people close to the situation.

Then it became El Dorado
And you couldn't tell the Vandals from the Huns from
The president of Liberia waving to the president of Gabon
Across the Gulf of Guinea.
And you sure the hell didn't want them remembering
The Golden Rule when they came to
Or wherever their final punctuation may have taken them.

When wombed summer kicked late but hard
It was the Silver Dollar-Sized Pancakes Drive-In.
We watched that hot surrender scene over and over,
Drinking hoof fluid by the acrefoot.
Green grew the Cadillacs
Like laboratory rats,
Ears running up and down their backs.

Discovery

Discovery

My name is Gray, and you will lerne stuff about me.
Things that I em good at is Math also Legos,
game boy and nintedo.
I'm bad at Rreding and ratihing.
I've accomplished the pigrim,
Evry nitedo game I have: and all the grad's up to 4 grad.
In the future I'd like to be a game boy and nintedo maker.
I hope you lernt about me.

Kentucky

Morning incants the stables,
Steam geniis from buckets,
Bodies haughty and slicked like seals,
A pride of oils, ointments, soaps,
Sultry thoroughbreds in greatcoats, fragile
Dancers' legs wrapped in sexy hot colors.

Critiquing the caliber of the company--
No wind, no heart--
The tobacco chewing, beer-bellied ballet master
Doubling as the track paramedic.
The young guys like to be out picking up bleeding bodies.
He did that for 14 years. He don't need that shit anymore.

With a double and an exacta nested in my wallet
Like yellowjackets in the aluminum siding
I paid homage to the poet laureate,
Shopped for the cats because I knew
They'd be waiting for me in their black smoking jackets.
The gas station owner's running for Jailer.

In the morning, yesterday lingers like pin oaks and maple.
What a plain ordinary jerk I am,
Like something hidden in three measures of Mail Pouch
In this Kentucky of Robert Penn Warren
And Piggly-Wiggly
And Race-Trac gas.

Putting Descartes Before The Whores

You can't hurry love
And so it takes forever to get there.
Block upon block like pop-up books
Opening to pink and lemon-scented Derridas
Tufted young toughs from Tufts
All You Can Eat Menudo,

Yakkety yak the Heideggerian streetcars go,
Althusserian macaques hail cabs.
Machiavellian crews
Baudrillard down the boulevard
In love with blue on a map of the world,
Like Wittgenstein in search of ever-bigger game.

Relatively no time goes by.
I drop Socratic anchor
Somewhere between the combat zone and
The Boutique Of Pure Reason.
The ½ Japanese, ½ Mexican proprietress
Stands behind a case of mistaken identity,

Tarsier eyes wide and peeled for Blad Peet,
To ensnare him with a bit of Kant,
A snatch of Schopenhauer
And breasts of chocolate pecan turtles.
Suckers work hard, fools play by the rules.
That's *her* philosophy.

Arts and Lectures

A six-pack, some weed,
Eventually
You get tired of it
For breakfast
Every day.

Seeing things others don't?
No, just the opposite.
My windows are covered with arts and lectures brochures.
The light of the liquid ambers seeps through
And I'm reading Myth Hamilton's Edithology.

Possessing powers others don't?
On the contrary.
I can't sleep and the food bank doesn't open until 10.
And I wouldn't know how to get there and back
If not for my addictive personality.

It used to be for a pack of cigarettes at the liquor store
Now it's for plywood at Home Depot
That Zeus comes back a week later from.
He drank himself into this situation.
Now, he'll have to drink himself out of it.

Or to put it another way
The arts and lectures series at the university is all
Late bloomers, lute
Blamers, thesis exhibitors
On paid administrative leave.

Last week
A blind duck
Flew head first into
A duck blind,
This week it's whoever has the biggest mouth.

Merced Beauties

I flew at the pork chops
And my glasses flew
Right off my head.
I grunted and farted
Like I was devouring tarmac,
Altarpieces by the fistful.

I like to growl and yip and snort over my food.
With a permanent scowl of you goddam right.
They put me in the back of the restaurant
Past even where the help eats.
Where Cooties with proboscis collapsed like telescopes eat.
The only ease I ever feel is ill at ease.

The twins take me for all I'm worth.
They are like licking a 9-volt battery.
Their gang portrait hangs in the kitchen.
Any Tuesday can be Monday
But rarely is Thursday Friday
In eluding the multidisciplinary team.

Men whose names begin with Z
Are most at risk for heart trouble.
For instance, Zorro.
I see the twins left their sexy underwear by the keyboard.
Margaritas were spilt,
A bucket of chicken.

I sleep in the sewing room/computer room/guest bedroom.
My body like a Z on the daybed.
I lull myself to sleep counting vicious beatings
I administer to those who train children and dogs to kill.
My lawyer is a public defender
But the public is indefensible.

Team 10 Coverage

I live in a mid-sized special effects house.
Thanks to the glorious techniques for vaginal tightening,
And bikini waxing,
I am very popular in Thai Town and Little Italy.
My name is Korean for "Smokes like Shostakovich."
Teutonic for "What did you expect?"
Celtic for "Well, that's over."
Sanskrit for "Drunk or no, I was right when I wrote to Neil
THE question is:
Does a quip have a place in today's crossword puzzle?"

The results came back from the lab.
The clouds tested positive for pink.
The second opinion was worse than the first.
I should have known not to cross my chickens
Before they counted the street.
What would you do if I were me?
What would I do if you were me?
Waiting for that special *noche de foam finger,*
When the Lord's minutes are anytime minutes.
Team 10 Coverage begins now.

Sometimes I Confuse Azaleas With Sibelius

Sunrise and I'm already drinking like it's the full moon.
Bowing to the house.
Leading by example.
A terrible example of an enfant terrible.
The Maestro gesturing to the orchestra.
Sometimes I start out conducting somebody's 5th
Only to discover it's really somebody else's 3rd.

More than once it wasn't until the 7th
Beer that I even realized I'd been drinking
Let alone approaching scherzo cum finale.
And Mahler's 6th is my family's theme song.
Sometimes I confuse azaleas with Sibelius
But I schedule my concerts to coincide with my laundry.
And where does it say in The Bible

And a Finnish boy shall lead them?
The philharmonic is basically a cover band
They could easily be playing weekends at Black Angus.
You've got to make the Mexican girls scream,
Esa-Pekka *Mentiras,* you've got to break their hearts.
I'll tell you what.
Let's have a couple of *cervezas.*

Norms

Living proof of living proof,
Diapered oxen yoked at the nostrils to oxygen tanks
Eyes armed to the teeth with pain
Or otherwise signified by
Old promotional clothing from the thrift store free box.
Funny ducks walking with walkers
A jargon of bonescans and swallow tests and chest x-rays
Some don't know who they are anymore.

Her voice is a front yard of cactus and gravel,
Her breasts terra cotta pots.
She's balancing a four-Ferris Wheel weekend and
A cop is planted in the booth behind me and
I'm higher than a kite and
Reading the newspaper like it is
An emergency exit plan
Written in Chinese.

The pictures are sharp on recycled papyrus
Colorful 2nd Armored Cavs leapfrogging ecumenical cairns.
A Chihuahua trampolining across the Champlain Valley.
The B-52's at Wit's End.
Drug deal at the park-and-ride.
Kidnapped calendars, postmodern ransoms
Smoking bullets ejaculated from silver guns
Deserts falling like Berlin Walls to off-road vehicles

My inner hep-cat shifts into mojo supreme.
My mind drifts like winged seed
And that's what we mean when we say
Intent is 18/twentyfirsts of the law
Where there are more people hoping to die at home
Who don't have a home
And more miniature golf holes per capita
Than anywhere else in the world.

Near The Whiting Bros. Ruins

Ochre and copper, the sky.
I was trying to alibi a called third strike.
"Things will reveal themselves to you,"
The spiritual advisor megaphoned.

Dad got snagged on a jetty jack crossing the Rio Grande.
Mom beat the insurance company.
That's the money I'm drinking Old Milwaukee at the
Tomahawk Bar with.

The last time I saw Dad he was snot-dripping weeping,
Drinking morphine like it was Mountain Dew.
The last time I saw Mom was at some
Suspension bridge or summit or continental divide.

Bereavement ends at the point of
Electronic confirmation of a transfer of funds.
And I've got the death certificates and receipts to prove it.
Eternal grace? I'd settle for a two-week grace period.

Or another beer and a breakfast burrito.
Brain surgery and a lube job.
Reservation Prices.
And the sun is so low my tattoos throw shadows

If Not For Love, Then Why?

Gather.
Hunt.
A little weaving,
A little fishing,
And then the son of a bitching Spaniards arrive
And all of a sudden it's U.S. Highway 101.

A tortured lake,
A stand of black bamboo,
A grocery clerk emoting plans,
A mayhem of drumming nuns,
A humidor of sirens.
I'd seen it on t.v. waiting at the peach cobbler's

For him to finish my shoes.
He's like a clock with six second hands.
Shoes repaired While-U-Are-At-Prayer
Near where the El Salvadorans were executed
By a squad of Filipino clamshells.
Sound familiar? It should.

Like a conveyor belt of French cigars
And Cuban perfumes and Belarusian champagnes
Being scanned at the great Wal-Mart of China.
I've gone to my preferred premier priority reward club
Over and over again.
Anyone paying attention has.

Today was the five-year anniversary of
A lot of things that happened five years ago,
And every 40 seconds another friend
Of a friend gets somebody in trouble.
I watch the victims walking toward their doom
I know better, but I hope each time they will pull through.

La Enamorada

La Enamorada

Prettier than the very pretty 235 I bowled last night
She will steal your heart like
The night shift will steal your meds.
Enriched bread seemed sufficient
Until you heard about enriched uranium
Until you heard her say it in Spanish
And her beauty calls like an unexpected aircraft carrier:
Arms like the barrels of mint-silk muzzleloaders,
Legs like the *History of Civilization*
By Will and Ariel Durant.
Your mind becomes a dethroned king
Hiding amidst royal herds of mad cows.
For her life to alight upon you
For a minute, for a night,
Oh what you'd give to find a guard to bribe.

The High Cost Of Living

The grasshopper jumps onto an electrified fence.
Fireworks of flaming wings
Flaming legs,
Flaming head,
Flaming abdomen segments.

Igniting the dry grass like
Methamphetamine-crazed brides, gowns aflame.
Rocks pop like champagne.
Trees come apart at the seams.
When I am with you I am the grasshopper.

Life is not meant to be examined
Just stared at,
Like the RCA Victor dog
Staring into the bell of Dizzy Gillespie's trumpet
All "Fuck my Master's voice, what is *this* shit?"

It'll say one thing right to your face
Something completely different
Right to your other face.
Like Tutsis choosing Tagalog at the ATM
Just because they can.

America's Sweetheart

The bus driver is a banana
On the bluebonnet route
To the gingerbread clinic,
A face like the big flower
That squirted anybody trying to smell it
That I wore on my clown prince costume
When I skated all over the world.
In Holiday On Ice.
I have a picture of me
With America's Sweetheart.
The one who almost o.d'd.
You heard about it.
It was pretty iffy there for a while.
But she's out of the woods now.
The woods told her
Get the fuck out of here.

Time grunts like intake workers
Barks like a retired show dog.
Wheat colored igloos kiwi the peach amphitheatre
Which is to say: dawn.
And in the squeamish half-light
Of the coffee shop
Outpatients from the inner city
And others discharged at 2 a.m.
Who *are* the better players of Beethoven string quartets:
Germans or Japanese?
We are, she says looking at her reflection in the window.
She says she wants a face-lift.
Them woods are beckoning her back.
She wasn't really, she wanted to be
America's Sweetheart
I wanted her to be, too.

Velocity

The taste of her remains, a pool in the cavern of my throat.
Winter in Vancouver, eye contact at the bookstore,
She was coming out, I was going in,
That night Peru and China went at it machete and sickle.

Her skin as white as pampas plumes
As firm and supple as wind instruments made of wind
Asesino! Asesino! she screams as I swipe her
Like a hyper-consumer at the point of sale.

Velocity is not only speed, she is also direction.
Constant speed in a constant direction.
She knew how to dare you to make it dangerous.
She can't help it, her body hands her over.

Her Periodic Table contains only the element of surprise.
One minute she's straddling you
Like a cooling tower at a nuclear plant
And the next she's taking it in the concession stand.

Acceleration is another whole rate of change,
A perspectivist cool with excursions into different keys,
One arm a crescent moon around my neck
The other drifting in slow motion pleasure,

The way she melted like a wedding white convertible top.
And as any tollbooth operator on a dark, flurrying night,
Or bullet-head physics professor can tell you,
The greater the Velocity the more profound the kill.

Mademoiselle Is Very Picky About Her French Fries

"Supposing truth is a woman---what then?"
                                        Nietzsche

The night of the folding chair air force
And a perfectly positioned cricket
Swears me off Japanese fiction.
And physically repulsive leaders.
Too many zeks gave their lives
Not to understand the reason why
Mademoiselle is very picky about her French fries.

If it's not the container, then it's the serving size,
Or the cut. She don't like old, cold, or soggy.
In fact she is very picky about everything.
She requires not only good genes
But particular alleles at particular loci.
For you it's a rite, for her a routine
Right there in the *fronteriza.*

Emerald incense, matches of midnight blue,
The serifs of her hair like black fire.
From the Tasmanian shampoo.
Fresh and hot, exactly the way she likes her fries.
And a new Fines Doubled For Speeding zone
Whenever she needs a new pursuit,
Particular officers at particular speeds.

When The Rain Is Caged

When the rain is caged, only then will I go to the zoo.
And when the pensioners' circus comes to town
Oh don't set a mockingbird near a riffing wren,
Soon enough will the fledges be swept.

I ran like an owl to the drugstore, exuviating all the way.
The girl behind the counter,
Skin whiter than dictionary paper,
Hair like rusted sand, eyes like blue Spanish tile.

It may surprise you to hear this, but
If Mother Nature were human, she'd be dead.
The things we did.
Avian melee

The psychiatric industry calls it.
Some people kill themselves because they can't take it.
Some break out in hives.
Some never learn.

Some come from good but foolhardy stock.
Some get on my nerves so bad
I want to rob a Burger King
And eat a chicken sandwich while I'm doing it.

Portlandia

I love hoarse and rough-cut chicks,
Dyed hair, black clothes, matchbook smiles,
Products of lingerie and transfer points,
Passports are i.d. in their own neighborhoods,
And then before we know it,
We never make it to the museum.

But being a distinguished visiting fellow
The fact that $(a^2-b^2) = (a + b) \times (a - b)$
Means we're playing croquet indoors at dawn
Although I don't do well at games
As I've learned the karma of not rooting against others.
And I sip my tequila, too. I don't shoot it.

And when structuralist views start getting me down
Portlandia in tank top and baggy shorts brings out
The ludic in me.
And before we know it there's a mattress in the fast lane
And it won't be until that evening
That the morning paper gets read.

The Date

She drank like an adult child of alcoholics
Who never drank but *exhibited* the tendencies.
She is white as a pastry bag and only 1/64th
But she *exhibits* the tendency.
I thought she was a butcher or sold cosmetics
Turns out she does drug tests, handles other people's pee.

You, to the end zone, do you want to rush with me?
We pass teething priests collecting doors for the doorless,
Two high functioning cabooses fighting over a bitch.
The dining room rises over the city like a whale's fluke.
We both had the braised tropes served on a bed of codicils.
And we drove to my place in a paparazzi of paper cranes.

Her nail polish is the color of spent nuclear reactor rods.
But her hands could take the tension out of a cat's eye.
Her mouth is crowbarred in ecstasy
Just before she disintegrates like a jigsaw puzzle.
They don't call me Billy Two-Frames for nothing.
I'm very proud of several things we did on the date.

Introduction To Biology

"Instead of the thorn shall come up the fir tree…"
                                        Isaiah

About this business of making sow's purses out of silk ears.
So when the kids go crazy at ringside
As the albino tiger lady climbs through the ropes
At Wrestling While-U-Wait
Like it or not, it beats a boot camp haircut
Any old Neo-Platonist baggage-screening day.
Forget about what's happening on Level 3.

My baby's Yemeni honey skin tone
Comes from a legal pad padded tanning booth.
Oh how I love caressing the swanny thigh of the hollow leg
That reservoirs the atomic lava she gulps
From the see-through sows' ears.
Her silk purse contains a cell phone and tanning lotion.
It's all on her say-so, anyway.

I remember the time she went up for a slam dunk.
Our jaws dropped like baby giraffes.
Or the time she stabbed a neighbor with her dibble,
The one she'd gotten at a garage sale
And then juked him
For laughing at her sow's silk purse.
We even got some of that say-so on us.

No matter the savannah
Or silky the sow or eerie the purse
Or how much your town's economy depends upon
The state hospital for the insane
98 percent of heat loss in the neighborhood is due
To the hate bubbling behind her father
And she has his eyes.

The Switched Order

The order got switched: she got the extra
Bacon, he got the embroidered chasuble,
And I got stuck with the child support and alimony.
Where's Bud? I yelled.
In walked Bud, and all was well.
Twice the man and three times the woman
I am, she is
The quintessential quintesexual,
Smooth as a tapered candle.
Memory serves but you still have to tip.

Everybody digs the pink-jacketed horn player.
The guitarist doing long division with his axe,
The sax kicking like an existentialist gale,
Or a fighter and his publicity photo fists,
And some secret agent man riffs.
The piano player burns crop circles in the sound system,
His fingers like hot larks sparkling off crushed rock,
And the bass is a *paseoperros,*
With the muscle memory of a fedayeen,
Until the front man returns at an oblique angle.

She who is not with us is he who is against us
And the order got switched again.
Bud and the horn player became one
Leaving me to twist it in like a socket wrench.
Ooooh you tip so good, the waitress moaned.
Well, I corrected.
Well AND good, she double corrected
And snapped like a bear trap.
Mission bells rang like they were swatting flies.
A discourse of informed trajectories dashed from the trees.

Simpatico Patio!

Simpatico Patio!

I have a show! Do you?
Do you have a show, too?
Then there's a pair of us—don't tell!
They'd envy us, you know.

How dreary to not have a show!
How nobody, like a frog
To have your name the livelong day
Unknown to an admiring bog!

Simpatico Patio! is the name of my show.
People join me on my patio.
Simpatico people!
Patio furniture!

Summer Ought One

It takes 17 muscles to smile and 43 to frown,
But it only takes an hour and a half to get to Los Angeles.
The flight was deep and ponderous and rich with
Imagists in from as far out as Peppermint Odes.
Somebody held a simile to my head.
I remember it like it was tomorrow.

A bitter owl to swallow at the time:
Not wise enough to be a philosopher.
*"Laden with honors on both sides of the Rhine."**
They invented the dot on digital clocks for me.
Can't tell p.m. from the Fauve period.
So I sought the *next* least remunerative career possible.

Default is often in the stars,
A blessing in the skies,
Fuck what your ticket says.
Plan B should have been Plan A from before the git go.
"Are you nuts?" she squirmed, pushing me away.
"You are *escrewed* up."

Tires grip the road in a Robt. Wms. kind of way.
It's either the cops or Pizza Hut
And nobody ordered pizza.
A story older than time itself:
The cruise singer who never leaves the ship
And the naturalist who loves him.

Dawn dawns just before dawn,
Snapping my mind like it was a desert prospector's,
Flipping it crisply like slot machines or asterisks.
Futurist, Dadaist---I eschew all labels.**
I eschew because it's true: I really <u>am</u> *escrewed* up.
Are you with me Dr. Tulp?
...

Zulu and Mameluke cleave and calve like
Argentinean beeves hanging like tobacco
From red Chinese roofs,
Loosely, like the cotton tank top
Monique sleeps in so as not to catch it on her
Post-Marxist nipple piercing.

*I want it said of me: "He visited Schwitters in Hanover."
**I want it said of me: "He's an *eclectic* em-effer."

"Dinner?" she sneered

Daddy Gibbon gives the *grito* from a double-decker
Bus spewing black labcoat ghosts.
I'm on my way to replenish
Day after day my one good year.

I captured the imagination of a reading public.
It didn't take a bird of paradise to tell me
I was in paradise, it had to be paradise
My shit didn't stink and my piss glittered like a sombrero.

I was great friends with girl jockeys
And a different actress each time accompanied me
And whoever so cool I was at the jazz club with
Maceo Parker had to leap from the stage to blow us a rift.

But shit shifts in flight
And tumbles out of the overhead storage bins
Like infants pitching from residential hotel cribs
In the Mexican section of Berlin.

 "I want the literary world's respect," I tell the new cashier
A suicidal party girl mad at her dad.
"And not only respect---I want an outpouring."
She drags the bottle over the scanner like a bum leg.

In my room it could be Perth,
It could be Ouagadougou.
It could be Anne-Sophie Mutter.
Can you read me? Can anybody read me?

Happiness

Had I been born in 1935,
My dad would have been an 8-year-old father
And in the summer of 1957 I'd be
Inhaling the juniper fresh air of existentialism,
My book of poems just out from Nude Erections.

Not so much poetry as prose hockey.
A power play of desert marigold and Vicks Vapo rub,
Van Gogh at the Los Angeles Municipal Art Gallery
At Vermont Avenue and Hollywood Boulevard.
The d.j. was from Dijon

And playing a Well-You-Needn't-A-Thon.
Hooray for parents who name their daughters Desiree!
She said neurosis; I thought she said blue roses.
Her beauty would mean
Death to a millennium-zero theologian.

I'm proud of the fact that I'm the son of one in a million.
I'm happier than Cage coaxing sound from late rent.
Although I hope to come to by Sunday
It's not really my place
To make those kinds of dreams come true.

Saddle Tramp

The wine tastes like lead-based paint.
And stinks like a Sunday morning shit in the half bath.
Inheritance is a death sentence, my dad said
So I studied with the greatest of Croatian composers.
That's why I'm wearing my lucky red underwear.
And I've got *Do Not Resuscitate* tattooed on my back.

Some days you are sacred, others game.
I made the switch to Elizabeth Bishop's *A Cold Spring*.
I would have been honored to carry her books,
So taking me to school did EB (still)
Just like I was honored to carry yours, and
The way I put my verso in your recto, it was manuscript!

But you turned out to be one more pretty girl Floyd,
And I became a saddle tramp again, riding the poetry range.
Writing about what I don't know,
Because everybody else is writing about what they do,
Like they all were spat from the same
Whorebitch who made that California trip.

Fallen Hero

And the surfing cowboy shooting the pier
In bearskin coat and beaver mittens
Chased out of Memory Park by
Mesquite-flavored international relief workers
Calling out in his sleep like the three-eyed sheep
Bleating for its mother,
Her nose, her thirteen fingers, her five feet
On the street that runs counter to
What passes for parallel to
A center of gravity vulnerable to
Reciprocating mass
Not far from where a girl was murdered like a starlet
Stabbed to death by north arrows.

Carnival workers are kicking it at the stupa
Behind the Surfin' Chicken Jr.,
Eyes red from the karma floats made with real karma.
Miss Black Sacramento winks
Because she knows where there is no Africa
Tarzan perishes.
No Future Embryo Farmers Of America are there
Sending millions of frozen imposters to Bavarian castles.
Some call it martyrdom.
I call it tough fucking shit,
A chariot pulled by a kangaroo.
Lucky I've got enough meth and Maker's to see
Me through

Best Western

We are a couple of wildlife documentary filmmakers
Have you had enough, darling?
I have not, sweetheart.
Would you like more, darling?
Yes, that would be wonderful, thank you sweetheart.
Bottle opener screwed into the vanity.

Dr. Jack was the house physician.
Furniture dimpled with cigarette burns,
Venetian blind ends creased from peering out to the street,
Where when you give me something
In my mind you have saved me the bother
Of having to steal it from you.

In your mind it makes me beholden to you forever.
A storm hits at midnight.
An upset in the Derby.
Spanish whispered into my ear all night long.
Won the roses.
On a sloppy track.

The next morning the mirror does not favor the original.
Teeth missing, funny marks,
The pallor of a cheap smoke detector.
Raindrops race each other like words down the window,
Reflected, tunneling up the paper like words,
The woman of her dreams still asleep.

The ashtray says Best Western.
And the doctor saw me right away.
Soon I was drinking my binoculars
Watching her wake,
A profusion excessive and non-native,
Needing only 5 to 30 minutes of sleep in a 24-hour period!

There's One In Every Crowd

As a kid I playacted being an addict.
The allure of utter abandonment to pleasure
Was better than being an astronaut.
The utter futility of losers was thrilling.

I threw in with the Confederacy, the Soviet Union,
I sought physical defeat and intellectual decadence,
Bloody maulings and bloodier ravagement.
And it's been pretty much a dream come true,

The affinity for disfigurement
For the sake of the art.
No wonder I became a poet.
I'm good at what I do

I write to make the tingling in my arms less urgent,
The tightness in my chest less ominous,
The high-pitched whistling in my ears of shorter duration,
The knife blades opening in my ass less painful.

Jury Duty

Jury Duty

Well, it's now good afternoon
I've been busy so I couldn't e-mail back this morning
Yes since I did get picked for jury duty I got behind.

This was my first time on jury duty
It took only 3 days so it wasn't so bad
'cause it's taken longer sometimes

and mine was a misdemeanor for a 20-year-old guy
it was for drugs so I thought he was guilty based on
the evidence and him not wanting to take three tests

so he didn't leave many doors open for himself I guess.
When all the jurors came in to decide on the verdict
(by the way I was juror #2)

We all went to a conference room
and we looked at all the pros and cons
and all 12 of us jurors

We all decided he was guilty
so we sentenced him.
But it's O.K.

Cause he was not going to go to jail or anything
It's the guy's first try so he was just going to be on
probation and go to counseling

I think that is good for him
so now he can think back
and not do it again.

A Brief Detour

Reflected in honeycomb cells of high-rise windows
The evidence was irrefutable:
It sucked not to be us.
Any peanut-haired, French-manicured barista knew that.

Cleansed of God by our parents
We cleansed ourselves of history,
Genius coded in our natural, cardholder's instincts.
Like heroin, time and gravity, plentiful and cheap.

Then the magic carpets flew into the teeth of the ostrich.
The Check-Mart Republic shit its capitalist thong.
Hissing like cockroaches mad for hot mummy:
"Everything has changed."

Oh say our star spangled banners
Popped up like car trunks
As sure as addicts return
Like swallows to the methadone clinic.

Soon daddies returned
Comparing cell phones like penises
And mommies returned
To taking their babies a bath.

Freedom

Some are dying of hunger in Harare,
Some are dying of exposure in Hong Kong,
Some are dying of hunger and lack of exposure in
Hollywood.
Me? I'm a big fat pig with a big fat smile on my face.
Smell me, smell my freedom.

I smell of freedom in my mouth.
I smell of freedom in my ears.
I smell of freedom in my armpits.
I smell of freedom in my nostrils.
I smell of freedom in my ass,
Where you want to smell of freedom the most.

You want to reek of it.
Like the reign of Otto Palindrominous
He knew when to meld, he knew when to smell.
You, too, can live in a Palace Of Freedom.
You, too, are a foot-dipping multipedal personality.
So start step right upping and smelling of freedom

Freedom smells like janitors rallying over contract talks.
Freedom smells like honeymooners in Hawaii.
Freedom smells like a customized PIN.
X marks the fjord when it comes to freedom.
When you smell of freedom, you smell *good*,
I don't care what anybody says.

Deliver Us From The Housing Authority

She gets off the bus a stop before the regular school stop.
He waits for her every morning.
They barely look at each other.
Two magnets at the magnet school.
Stroking each other like local celebrities.
And then behind the cafeteria making out like bandits.

One of those sons' girlfriends a mother never gets to know,
Somebody's cousin in the corner getting high.
Her mother's junkie boyfriend's name
Is the same as her dad's.
A junkie killed her dad.
She slips off-center, like a funeral director's hairpiece.

Junk mail comes addressed Valued Lunatic.
She goes out with guys in construction.
Swallowing ottoman after ottoman.
Or else she knew them from AA.
Primo Meridian she met in the psycho ward.
We hooked up when they hooked up Primo to life support.

And lead us not onto the short bus
But deliver us from the housing authority.
For thine is the six-pack,
And the pit bull,
And the food stamps,
Forever.

Whispers From The Undercroft

Never more than a baker's dozen at the services:
From the lofty organist to
Father Ludwig,
Taking communion like goldfish.

A fog of incense
Laying on of hands
The body like a mural
Anointed with oil.

There were whispers from the undercroft.
And when the organist lost his loftiness
They plugged him in like the device you plug into the
Cigarette lighter that gives six more cigarette lighters.

Oh just a little errata in your giddyup, everyone said.
But they knew the field had been harvested
And the sheep had gleaned.
And it terminated in a black-keyed dirge.

Like A Dance In A Barbed Wire Foyer

The time comes to examine your own tortillas.
Message in a bottle says get out while you can
Because in time of war the price of hot meat skyrockets
And you end up taking nourishment through the eyes,
Like a dance in a barbed wire foyer,
Cinderella leaving behind her glass jaw at the ball.
What was I *supposed* to do
--a little Japanese bow to the beer in the fridge?--
In order to right that wrong, that ship?

Heartsick assets,
Monkeys drunk as ruddy hummingbirds,
Navajo girls abandoning their kindles
Bloody there and home,
Fresh 3-year-olds killing themselves,
Shooting themselves with daddy's gun
Or licking up daddy's cocaine
Daddy get mad.
Mommy get mad, too.

Gratuitous News

He wished upon a star,
Then washed his hands of the whole affair.
I was going to say that sounds a little wishy washy
But the way his hands shook,
The wings of a fly coming to,
When he had to use his tie to guide the cup to his mouth
Without spilling,
Everyone I've ever known from there has been nuts.
It's the substance of things joked for,
The impudence of things obscene.

And even though creative dispute resolution is all the rage,
That led to gunplay at Sonny Aker's.
The cop whipped a bitch from the wrong end
Of the irradiated opera glasses his windshield had become.
A dozen dachshunds came out with their ears up.
I have passports and wedding pictures to prove it.
The suspect tried sneaking out the Eastern time zone
But he slipped on the color-coded keyboard.
Put *that* in your journal or whatever it is you write what
You want to remember down in.

That Goes For The Queen Of Thai Silk, Too

Ride the MACRO to the sweat lodge
Of the building some guy is pissing against
While his little boy pees into the gutter.
In any other world that would have been the clincher
But we don't clinch here.

It was the corpse I was embarrassed for,
Hanging by its neck in a noose at the end of a rope
Attached to the trestle of the bridge,
Hanging solitary in a backlight of empty space
Covered like milkweed with caterpillars

And the emergency vehicle lights rouging the scene
Red like the auditorium
You were there.
You know what it's all about.
There's no getting past it,

Nor the snowy egret at the entrance
Collecting for the poor
Where the inventor of what happens when you assume
A universal Palestine is speaking.
That goes for the queen of Thai silk, too.

And he must have seen the corpse.
But on the other hand maybe he was saying fuck you
To the roar of the very latest
And all the other sick shit I'm teaching you to turn your
Back to.

Separate Trips

I.

Bohemians with association fees,
Two by two,
Gal and gynecologist alike,
Vacationing hirsute and jolly,
Spooning Tibetan sherbet,
Ten days out and still no mutiny!
Parenthesis leaping like porpoises
Over a champagne tower of Y's
Served with aplomb by a liveried staff.
Is there anything more unforgettable than relaxing?

II.

The cruise liner is like white foothills behind the scows
And the waterfront cranes are milking container ships
As the sphinxes roar toward the international airport
Over the yards with Fresh Flowers and Hubcaps
And the big white blisters of isobutene across the street.
Ah, the aromas of burning fuel, rubber and fish.
If mama's inheritance money can
Keep us in vodka and weed,
Let's bask in the glow,
Crotchless panties, plastic fruit.

...

III.

There weren't as many cameras when Daddy Wags
Was a star, an All-Star,
The Most Valuable Player of the All-Star game.
Now you can die and go to hell
On account of being out of camera range.
Jack Kerouac said Los Angeles in the winter
Was a jungle compared to New York.
And Daddy Wags stayed excommunicated
Until the LA winter locked its jaw on him,
Like drowning in a wishing well.

The Max Planck Wrestling Team

The Max Planck Wrestling Team

This should be the shortest day of the year
But the Man Upstairs did a big flip-flop
And it turns out to be the longest day of the year.
Throw open your master bedroom window and you'll see
The Max Planck wrestling team,
All of them transistors.

There was a time when scientists dressed like scientists.
They attended colloquia
"Why shit simultaneously
Flows downhill and rises to the top like cream."
It didn't help matters, but it did help antimatters.
You can make a semi-conductor conduct, but not always.

A Good Communist Bookstore Clerk Is Hard To Find

Princes of the church,
Higher than bacteria counts,
Surf turd-morseled waves in cardinal wet suits.
The green room reeks like a public toilet
On the Lucerne to La Paz route.
Hang gliders leap from landfill peaks.
It's been going on for thousands of years
At the time this is being written,

A baby civilization espied in a sun-dried spectrometer.
Scholarly journals roam the Earth.
In the miniature Stonehenge dance
Girl on girl
Like lotus colored ice cubes
Tonged from silver buckets
5 million years ago
At the time this is being written.

The churros are charmed, but money mediates mañana.
Every evangelical enchilada and born again burrito
Knows that laughing faculty
Have been dragging their feet for a million years
At the time this is being written,
Getting natural in the last days,
Wearing their best x-rays over their clothes,
Leaving the public in stitches.

...

The war enters its 2 billionth year
At the time this is being written.
There's a communist bookstore
In the Brookings—Brazzaville corridor.
The clerk didn't know what I was talking about.
A good communist bookstore clerk is hard to find.
A bunch of boom mike lancers kicking it before
The fireworks would probably concur.

Activists Express Worry

Escaped alfalfa stinks like gang-related porcupine,
And Niagara Falls discharges cheesy algae blooms.
Diabetic rhinoceroses dance on their horns,
And whales suck butterscotch krill.
Vacuums abhor nature,
And I can back that up with my fists.

Indoor plumbing was humanity's apogee,
The telephone its biggest mistake,
Endangering already endangered vicuñas
Already flying too close to the ground,
Scattering flower petals and lipstick stained cigarette butts
From Maputo to the Massachusetts Institute of Technology.

Activists may express worry, but not me.
As long as women volleyball players
From beachfront universities
Anoint me with oil,
And mosquitoes with swollen brains and spinal cords
Purchase Danish furniture made in Singapore,

As long as my voice and data needs are being met,
Life is lightning in a bottle to me.
But wait—what's this?
A "best before" date
On a bottle of lightning?
I didn't think lightning could go bad.

What People Are Saying

The tequila's cheaper than gasoline
And she's drinking it like cough syrup
Because Pancho Bougainvillea
Ridden by that sappy-assed Pat Day
Got up and won the Belmont by a nose.
People say a lot of things.

They say Lincoln was gay
And Leary was a snitch.

You can't have too much tequila in you, she says,
In our love nest *cum* swing vote headquarters.
And with a driving finish we climax like baroque
In colonial Quito
After colonial Quito
After colonial Quito.

They say Mao's teeth were rotten
From too much sweet tea and poor home care.

The tequila is better than quark-gluon plasma,
And we're swinging like the golden age of
Famous cases from the annals of small-town psychiatry.
The only way I could be more in love
Is if she wrestled professionally under the name
Ayako Hamada.

They say it's not so much the evidence
As it is the magnitude of the charges.

...

All I know is nobody wants their pilot drinking
Tequila in the cocktail lounge ten minutes prior
To take off, or their girlfriend
On a first-name basis with every cab driver in town,
Or being reminded daily how quickly you'd be dropped
In favor of a member of the Arellano-Felix family.

They say in some cases
Your nearest exit is behind you.

You really can't have too much tequila in you,
Especially when the season you thought ran June to
November ends abruptly on Tuesday
And rain blackens the birds of paradise
And you're playing "Take Five" backwards
To hear: Paul is dead.

They say that rate is proportional to
The difference between the object and its surroundings.

This weekend the midget rodeo is in town
And there's Japanese women wrestling on t.v.
She's busy, and I'm drinking tequila like it's cough syrup.
People say a lot of things. All I know for sure is
Trotsky's getting blown by Frida one day,
Somebody's sticking an ice pick in his brain the next.

The Damned

This is some hard humming.
Kangaroo elephants leaping tree to tree
To get a better view of the
Civic light cockfights.
Cocks genetically engineered to steal Jewish assets from
Swiss banks.
Imagine the monkey business when it comes to humans!

And the news screens teem with
Chemically-altered Cains dying en masse like arroyo toads,
5-pound babies filling locomotive-size strollers
With Egyptian artifacts looted from British museums,
And body part harvests so bountiful
Pathologists pull down their barns and build greater.

It takes a village of the damned
To raise the children of the damned.
Consider the abbey cocooned with silly string,
An abbey chock full of abbots
Faces ashen, mouths agape,
Lost their bloody minds, don't know whom to thank.

Your Understanding Is My Understanding

Either we're as good as dead
Or like life on Mars
Not recognizing the hand.
And the primary language spoken in the home
Is very disappointing news.

History can play tricks on you.
Ask the Wizard of Oz.
Ask Oswald Spengler.
Ask Lee Harvey Oswald.
Ask Harvey Milk.

History generally regards my cousin to be the very
First guy to wear a hairnet out of his house.
Any other guy would have been killed.
But my cousin was such a dude
People left him alone.

My cousin had a light bulb for a heart.
He walked on water, especially in the desert,
And wore his heart on his sleeve
So he could see where he was going.
But between you and me

Thirty some people wanted are missing.
That's the extreme he was willing to go to.
There are a whole lot of right tracks one could be on.
Utrecht to Rome to Venice is one.
The reality of nothing is another.

Demands

It's not a dictatorship.
It's a nice family regime,
Siblings, in-laws, wives, mistresses and children.
Rhododendrons are the national anthem
And the national flower is the lotto.

And the national motto is whatever it is
When there's no money
To print ballots
And no money to print money.
They're robbing Peter to pay Rob.

I married a soy-brained native,
A cell phone through her nose.
We bought a condo
In the *quartier chinois* of the national capital
Where they kidnapped the Germans in absentia.

The fate of fate hangs in the balance.
Vote No on No.
Vote Yes on Never.
And how many statues of liberty should one nation have?
Tusked statues of liberty.

Or refugee busboys, or immigrant dishwashers?
It was the most Byzantine empire of any empire
Since the Byzantine Empire.
The emperor was not my biological father
But he was my illogical father.

And I realized
When they floated the posthumous parts downstream
Almost everybody is pretty
Much almost always making
Demands.

Who We Are, What We Believe Is More Fluid Than Ever

While the bass violin is on its side doing leg lifts
The French horn curls up in a handlebar basket
On destiny's runaway rickshaw
Swerving through the juried urban tundra
Of tricked-out prayers
And frozen steeds

In the glowering moonglow.
The streetclocks are bearded like tribal elders,
Black halos chucklingly honed against a stone of doubts.
Sword-bearing liberators
Maintain an icy street traffic
In candy and comic books.

"I think pooh pooh," says one panelist on t.v.
"I think pooh pooh, ca ca, pee pee," says another.
I think I wonder
What the Javanese villager
Who made the sweatshop thumbs
The panelists have got stuck up their asses thinks.

Crazy Like That

There went up a mist from the Earth
Like at a carwash on Saturday afternoon
And watered the whole face of the ground.
Food courts sprouted like prisons.
Mission Control unspooled.

Beekeepers and plumbing contractors,
Outplacement counselors and in-house experts,
Kiln manufacturers and black Persian Elvises,
All of us, leaning unto our own understanding
Not trusting in the Lord with all our hearts.

Now almost everybody's down to almost nothing.
Nobody asks if you want any
Because there isn't any.
Toll-free hotlines have been set up.
We're crazy like that.

Acknowledgements

"Bicycles, Bakers, and Cakes" is based on a dream my young nephew related to his mother.

Filmmaker "Luc Truffle" is the alter-ego (sort of) of filmmaker Neil Novello.

"Discovery" is an autobiographical statement by my young nephew.

"Sometimes I Confuse Azaleas With Sibelius" is a tribute to the Los Angeles Philharmonic and conductor Esa-Pekka Salonen.

The name "Portlandia" is taken from Raymond Kaskey's sculpture in Portland, Oregon.

Thanks to Tim and Terri of Write Up The Road for their friendship and encouragement.

About the Author

Born in Chicago, Randy Stark has also lived in Albuquerque, Seattle, and various locales in Southern California, including an architecturally-significant gas station in Venice. He graduated from the University of California, Santa Barbara, with a degree in cultural anthropology. His fiction and essays have appeared in literary magazines in the United States and Canada. This is his first book of poetry.

www.ingramcontent.com/pod-product-compliance
Lightning Source LLC
Chambersburg PA
CBHW031329040426
42443CB00005B/273